CW00859316

CH
OP

BEANS WITH SAUSAGE

ingredients

- 500 grams of beans
- sunflower oil
- 1 medium red onion
- 2 small peppers or 1 medium size
- 4 cloves garlic
- 1 medium tomato
- 150 grams of bacon
- 1 medium carrot
- 3 liters of water
- bay leaf (2 small or 1 medium)

- salt
- pepper
- 1 tablespoon Vegeta

- 6 pieces of sausage

For spray:
- 100 ml of sunflower oil
- 2 tablespoons plain flour
- 1 tablespoon ground sweet red pepper

instructions

1. The day before, soak the beans in water: transfer the beans to a bowl and pour enough water to cover the

beans.

2. Leave to stand overnight, preferably for 24 hours.

3. Strain the beans the next day.

4. Peel a red onion and cut it into small cubes.

5. Peel a squash, grate it and slice it.

6. Washed peppers cut in half and remove the stalk and seeds.

7. Peel the garlic and cut it into small cubes.

8. Peel a squash, grate it

and cut it into cubes.
9. Clean the bacon, and separate the skin from the rest.
10. Cut the rest of the bacon into strips.
11. Pour oil into a large pot on the stove to cover the bottom of the pot and let it heat up.
12. Add sliced onion to the oil, stir briefly, then garlic and stir briefly.
13. Add sliced carrots, stir, and peppers and stir again.

14. Then add sliced bacon and its skin. Stir to combine all ingredients.
15. Add diced fresh tomatoes and if you don't have fresh, you can use mashed tomatoes.
16. Stir well.
17. After that, add the strained beans, and pour 3 liters of water over everything.
18. Add the bay leaf.
19. Add salt, pepper

and Vegeta.

20. Cover and when it boils, cook over medium heat for 90 minutes.

21. For the spray, a special container must first be heated.

22. Then pour oil into it, let it heat up, then add flour.

23. Mix until everything becomes a homogeneous mixture and add the ground red pepper.

24. Fry everything briefly, put it in the beans and mix well.

25. Take a part of the bean liquid, mix the remaining powder in a bowl with it and pour everything into the beans.

26. Add sausages to the beans, which you previously pierce in a few places with a

fork.

27. Cook everything while stirring for another 15 minutes, then remove from the heat and serve while hot.

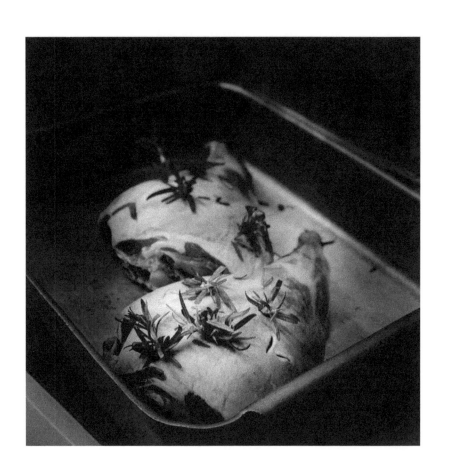

LAMB IN SCRAP

ingredients
- 2 kg of shoulder lamb with bones
- 8 medium-sized potatoes
- 1 larger head of red onion
- 8 cloves garlic
- 16 pieces of black olives
- 50 grams of dried tomatoes (can also be fresh cherry or grapolo tomatoes)

- 150 ml of red wine
- salt
- pepper
- 1 tablespoon rosemary
- olive oil

instructions

1. Separate the meat from the bones.
2. Part of the bones put to boil for soup.
3. Cut the boneless meat into larger pieces and set aside.

4. Peel the potatoes, wash and cut into quarters.
5. Put the potatoes to boil in the soup and when it boils, cook for 10 minutes.
6. During this time, clean the red onion and cut it into rings.
7. Peel the garlic and just cut the larger pieces in half.
8. Dried tomatoes also cut into smaller pieces,

and if there is no dried, then you can put fresh cherry or grapolo tomatoes cut in half.

9. After 10 minutes, remove the potatoes from the broth.

10. In a wide pan on the stove, fry the meat on all sides, stirring constantly.

11. When the meat has got a nice color, add sliced red onion.

12. Stir and add the garlic.
13. Stir again, and add the sun-dried tomatoes.
14. Mix the whole mixture.
15. Add salt and pepper.
16. Add the previously cooked potatoes and mix everything carefully.
17. Add olives, pour red wine, and add rosemary.

18. Let everything simmer for about 20 minutes, stirring occasionally.
19. During this time, prepare 4 baking sheets the size of a protvan from the oven.
20. Place an equal amount of the mixture together with the baking juice on all four pieces of paper and roll each piece of

paper on top so that it cannot be opened.
21. Place the scraps on the baking sheet.
22. Preheat the oven to 200 degrees Celsius and put everything in the oven for 50 minutes.
23. Rest the roasted scrap and serve the lamb on a plate with spring onions and radishes

MEAT LOAF WITH EGGS

ingredients
- 5 eggs (for filling)
- 850 g of mixed minced meat
- 1 bun (old)
- 100 ml milk (approx.)
- 2 eggs (for mixture)
- 1 onion
- chopped parsley
- salt

- freshly ground pepper
- butter to coat the mold
- crumbs
- oil

instructions

- Put eggs to boil.
- Cut the bun into smaller pieces, transfer to a larger bowl and pour over the milk to soften.
- Peel an onion and

cut it into smaller pieces and fry it in a pan with a little oil.
- Beat the remaining 2 eggs.
- Slice fresh parsley.
- Add beaten eggs, parsley, salt, pepper and onion to a bowl and mix gently.
- Add the meat and mix everything by hand.
- If the floor feels thin under your fingers, add

bread crumbs and mix everything well by hand again.
• Coat the inside of the mold measuring 30x11x7.5 centimeters with butter and sprinkle with bread crumbs. That way the loaf will get a nice shape.
• Fill the mold with half of the mixture.
• Peel the boiled eggs and arrange them on

the meat.
- Cover the eggs with the rest of the meat and make sure there are no holes in the meat.
- Turn the loaf out of the mold onto a baking sheet coated with oil.
- The loaf is baked in a preheated oven at 190 degrees for about 1 hour.
- Serve with mashed potatoes or roasted root vegetables

CHICKEN AND CHEESE STICKS

ingredients

- 400 g of Emmentaler cheese in one piece
- 650 g chicken breast or turkey breast white meat
- 5 tablespoons plain

flour

- 1 tablespoon ground red pepper
- 1 clove of garlic
- salt
- pepper
- 3 eggs
- 5 tablespoons bread crumbs
- 1500 ml of frying oil

For serving

- ketchup

instructions

- Cut the emmentaler into 8 equal pieces.
- Prick each piece of cheese on a wooden skewer stick.

- Fillet the chicken breasts and make long strips about 1 cm wide from each piece.
- Remove minor irregular pieces.
- Wrap the chicken strips around the cheese from top to bottom on all 8 pieces

and set aside.

- Slice the garlic and chop it.
- Mix flour, ground red pepper, chopped garlic, salt and pepper and mix everything well.
- Break the eggs, add a little salt and make

scrambled eggs.

- Cover each stick on all sides well with the prepared mixture.

- Then dip each stick into the eggs, then into the crumbs.

- Put the heated oil on a medium heat.

- When the oil heats

up, put two sticks in it so that the oil completely covers them.

- Fry over medium heat for 3 minutes.
- If left for longer, the cheese may leak out of the middle.
- Place on kitchen

paper to absorb excess fat from frying and serve warm with ketchup or some other addition to dishes such as mayonnaise or tartar. STICKS

CREAM OF MUSHROOM SOUP

ingredients
- 400 g mushrooms
- 50 grams of butter
- 1 medium-sized red onion
- 2 cloves garlic
- 3 tablespoons plain flour
- salt
- pepper
- 1.2 l of vegetable stock

- 200 ml of cooking cream

For serving
- fresh parsley
- golden soup balls
- sour cream

instructions

1. Peel the champignons and cut them into sheets about 3 millimeters thick.
2. Put them in a bowl.
3. Peel a squash, grate it and cut it into small

cubes. Remove from the side.

4. Peel a squash, grate it and chop finely.

5. Put butter in a deeper pan and heat it over medium heat.

6. Add onion and garlic to the heated butter and simmer, stirring, until glassy.

7. Then add sliced champignons and sauté them while stirring.

8. When the

champignons release the water, add the flour and mix everything well.

9. Everything will become a compact mixture.

10. Remove from the heat, then add the vegetable stock.

11. Stir and break up the cooking mixture.

12. Return the soup to the heat and when it boils cook for 20

minutes.

13. After that time, add the cooking cream, then cook for another 10 minutes.

14. Try the soup, and salt and pepper it as desired.

15. Pour the cooked soup into a plate, add sour cream and golden soup balls if desired.

MOUSSAKA WITH POTATOES AND MINCED MEAT

ingredients
- 1.5 kg of potatoes
- 1 larger onion head
- 600 g of mixed minced meat
- 1 tablespoon ground red pepper
- 2 eggs
- 2 sour cream
- salt
- pepper
- oil

instructions

- In a bowl on the stove put boiled potatoes in their skins, pour water over the potatoes and add salt.
- The potatoes are done when the fork passes lightly into it (I cooked for about 40 minutes).
- While the potatoes are cooking, peel the onion and cut it into small cubes.
- Heat a little oil in a

wide pan, add the onion and fry it over a medium heat.
• Then add the minced meat and sauté it, stirring constantly and dividing the meat into smaller pieces to make it loose.
• Add salt and pepper to the meat and mix everything again.
• Finally, add the red pepper, and mix it well with the mixture.

- Simmer for another 5 minutes, then set aside to cool.
- When the potatoes are cooked, drain them of water, let them cool for about 10 minutes, then peel them.
- After that, we will cut the potatoes into rings about 3 to 4 millimeters thick.
- Grease a 35x20 cm baking dish with oil, then stack the potato

rings partially on top of each other. In this way, arrange the entire row along the bottom of the protvan.
• The order of minced meat goes on the potatoes, being careful not to take a lot of liquid in which the meat was stewed.
• The potatoes should again be arranged on the meat in the same way as on the bottom

of the protvan.
- In a separate bowl, break the eggs, salt them and beat them briefly with a whisk.
- Then add sour cream to the eggs and beat everything again with a whisk.
- Spoon the egg and cream mixture over the potatoes.
- Bake the moussaka in a preheated oven at 200 degrees for 35 to

40 minutes.
• After baking, take it out of the oven, leave it to cool for about 15 minutes, and only then cut it.

CHILLI WITH MEAT

ingredients
- 4 tablespoons oil
- 1 large head of red onion
- 3 medium sized carrots
- 2 larger stalks of celery
- 500 grams of beef or mixed minced meat
- 6 cloves garlic
- 2 tablespoons ground sweet red pepper

- 1 fresh red pepper
- 400 grams of chopped canned tomatoes
- 500 ml of chicken or soup stock
- 2 small cans of red or brown beans
- a small can of corn
- salt and pepper as needed

instructions
1. Cook the soup stock

from the cube.

2. Cut the onion into cubes and set aside.

3. Peel a carrot and cut it into pieces.

4. Wash the celery stalk and cut it into pieces.

5. Peel a squash, grate it and slice it.

6. Peel and slice the washed red pepper,

7. Heat the oil in a large frying pan and add the onion.

8. Fry it over medium heat to become glassy.
9. Then add sliced carrots and celery and simmer.
10. After 5 minutes, add the meat and stir so that it does not burn.
11. When the meat has simmered add the garlic and ground sweet red pepper (since I'm not an excessive fan of hot

peppers, I didn't add hot peppers, and you are free to put it to taste).

12. Mix everything well, then add sliced red pepper and fry it briefly while stirring.

13. Add chopped tomatoes to the pan, mix everything well and pour over the stock.

14. Cook for about twenty minutes on

medium heat.

15. Towards the end of cooking, add beans and corn to the pan.

16. Add salt and pepper to taste.

17. Cook until the liquid has completely evaporated.

Lightning Source UK Ltd.
Milton Keynes UK
UKHW021239260620
365570UK00001B/1/J